The Study:
Spiritual Action in Daily Life

Spiritual Action in Daily Life
THE STUDY

The Study:
Spiritual Action in Daily Life
Elizabeth A. Perry

Elizabeth A. Perry
2015

Copyright © 2015 by Elizabeth A. Perry

All rights reserved. This book or any portion thereof may not be reproduced or used in any manner whatsoever without the express written permission of the publisher except for the use of brief quotations in a book review or scholarly journal.

Scripture quotations are from New Revised Standard Version Bible, copyright © 1989 National Council of the Churches of Christ in the United States of America. Used by permission. All rights reserved.

First Printing: 2015

ISBN 978-0-578-16740-4

Elizabeth A. Perry
Post Office Box 227
New York, New York 10108

www.bethperry.net

Dedication

To all those who commit to openness, equality, creativity, and justice, in the church and in the world.

Contents

Acknowledgements	ix
Introduction	1
Week One	3
Week Two	11
Week Three	19
Week Four	26
Week Five	33
Week Six	41
Week Seven	48
Week Eight	56
Week Nine	62

Acknowledgements

I would like to thank everyone who has participated in the first versions of this study over the past few years! Your interaction, feedback, and support have been extremely valuable.

A special thank you goes to the individuals in ministry – clergy and laity – in my local congregation who allowed me to interview them and create the foundation for this study.

Elizabeth A. Perry

Introduction

In 2012, I volunteered to lead a Bible study. While my offer was warmly received, the reality was also shared: Wednesday nights worked for small group meetings but the building was already full!

My reply came without much thought: "So, lets do something digital." And The Study in its first form was born!

Appropriately, the testing phase of that first study took nine months! What developed was a simple system of text messages and podcasts (with a back-up website). I interviewed people in ministry at the church and created a podcast out of that interview with a short Bible study section at the end – 10 minutes total on average.

On Monday, I sent participants a text message with a link to the podcast; on Tuesday through Friday I sent a text message with a (hopefully) challenging question. Participants could text me back whenever they were moved to do that.

The first series of the study ran with two dozen people – and reran with another dozen. A second series ran with the same numbers. Including the trial participants, more than 60 people shared in the study – more than 40 unique individuals!

The Study

Some participants interacted daily, others occasionally, some not at all. But at all those levels people told me about how much the study meant to them!

So I began to wonder if there were more ways I needed to consider – and it is out of that wondering that the new version began – The Study: Spiritual Action in Daily Life.

Along with that version came the opportunity to create this book. It is based on the local church version – those two series of podcasts and text messages

The podcasts are not here, of course, nor are the parts that were personal to one congregation. But you will be reading the heart of the conversation that happened – as well as those challenging questions.

Unfortunately, you and I can't text message to discuss your thoughts or answers! But we can stay in touch – you can like the Facebook page for The Study: Spiritual Action in Daily Life. We can even have some limited public conversation there, if you'd like.

I hope you enjoy this book! And if you want to continue this type of study in community with others, be sure to sign up for the next running of The Study: Spiritual Action in Daily Life!

THE STUDY
Spiritual Action in Daily Life

Week One

... I have uttered what I did not understand,
things too wonderful for me, which I did not know...
I had heard of you by the hearing of the ear,
but now my eye sees you... - Job 42 (NRSV)

The Study

Meditation

The scripture for this week is from Job 38-42 – a long rant from God to Job. You can read any section of it and you'll get the message: Job doesn't know all there is to know!

Which is also good advice for all of us starting this – or any – study! But this long section also tells us that we can learn and change. While Job struggles (like many of us) to find God, God ultimately finds Job, which leads Job (and can lead us) to new ways of being.

It reminds me of Dorothee Soelle's writing in *The Silent Cry: Mysticism and Resistance:*

> "In the sense of theology that liberates, the soul that is united with God sees the world with God's eyes. That soul, like God, sees what otherwise is rendered invisible and irrelevant. It hears the whimpering of starving children and does not let itself be diverted from their misery, becoming one with God in perceiving and understanding as well as in acting. ...
>
> In liberating movements, the mystical eye sees God at work: seeing, hearing, acting, even in forms that are utterly secular. In the contingency of literacy programs, or collaboration in building a school, God's action is manifest. It is a mysticism

of wide-open eyes."

This week, we'll place ourselves where God might find us, keep our eyes wide open, see the world through God's eyes, and find new liberating ways of thinking, feeling, noticing, remembering, and acting.

Day 1

Look back over your own life with wide-opened eyes: where has God been searching for you?

_____
_____
_____
_____
_____
_____
_____
_____
_____
_____
_____
_____
_____
_____
_____

Day 2

Job's losses caused grief and righteous anger. What might you learn from him to help you cope with any similar feelings?

The Study

Day 3

Do you notice any whirlwinds around you today? What might that whirlwind say to you?

_____
_____
_____
_____
_____
_____
_____
_____
_____
_____
_____
_____
_____
_____
_____

Day 4

Bread symbolized the good in Job's later life. What do you think might symbolize the good in your life today?

The Study

Day 5

Dorothee Soelle says that a liberating reading of the Bible is the answer to what afflicts human beings… What might you do today to bring that liberating reading into the world around you?

THE STUDY
Spiritual Action in Daily Life

Week Two

*Greet Prisca and Aquila, who work with me in Christ Jesus,
and who risked their necks for my life,
to whom not only I give thanks,
but also all the churches of the Gentiles.
Greet also the church in their house. – Romans 16:3-5 (NRSV)*

The Study

Meditation

This week's scripture – in fact, all of Romans 16 and the majority of the Epistles! – give us great insight into the diversity of the ancient church!

There were men and women. Some of each gender were married, some were single; some apparently led stable lives, others moved and traveled.

Ethnically, they were extremely diverse. Among the Gentiles were Prisca and her husband Aquilla, who were Romans. Nympha was Greek, as was Philemon. Among the Jews were Paul, Peter, and many others.

There was also broad diversity of ages: 2 Timothy 1:5 describes three generations in faith: son, mother, grandmother!

No wonder the church was growing so fast! Think of all those sources for evangelism – all those ways to reach new people! What would happen in our churches today if we began to see the diversity of early church membership as our highest goal? And what if we saw diversity as a goal for our individual lives as well?

This week, we'll look for places we can honor the diversity that already exists in our lives, families, neighborhoods, and spiritual communities.

And we'll also look for places where we could build more diversity! We might even find a few of those dark places where we try to avoid diversity and ponder what Jesus might say to us there.

The Study

Day 1

What is your earliest memory of diversity in a spiritual community?

Day 2

Christians even diversified where they worshipped: from house church to cathedral to chapel to auditorium! As you go about your life today, check out your environment: how might your worship happen there?

The Study

Day 3

What is your favorite intergenerational activity in your spiritual community? Do you see God's presence there? What need does it fill in your spirit?

_____

_____

_____

_____

_____

_____

_____

_____

_____

_____

_____

_____

Day 4

Who are the Prisca and Aquilla, Nympa and Philemon, of your spiritual community? How can you thank them for bring diversity and faith into your spiritual life?

_____
_____
_____
_____
_____
_____
_____
_____
_____
_____
_____
_____
_____
_____

The Study

Day 5

Where is diversity lacking in your faith/work/home community? What can you do to build diversity there today?

_____
_____
_____
_____
_____
_____
_____
_____
_____
_____
_____
_____
_____
_____
_____
_____

The Study
Spiritual Action in Daily Life

Week Three

Let all the inhabitants of the land tremble...
Like blackness spread upon the mountains,
a great and powerful army comes...
Then afterwards I will pour out my spirit on all flesh;
your sons and your daughters shall prophesy,
your old men shall dream dreams,
and your young men shall see visions.
Even on the male and female slaves, in those days,
I will pour out my spirit. - Joel 2 (NRSV)

The Study

Meditation

I interviewed a pastor once about his views on prophecy… and he told me all about the zombie apocalypse! Perhaps you read both scripture and zombie genre but, if not, let me tell you, there's an end time connection to the two!

Our worst fears come to the surface in both, our darkest ideas about death and the life beyond it. The army devours life and the source of life – be they locust or zombie soldiers. The waves of death bring us to our knees until we are little more than death ourselves.

But – and this is a big "but" - there is also a promise in the apocalypse – even in the zombie apocalypse and much more in scripture. Once those worst fears are realized, once the army has passed, then the blessings abound!

When you tie the apocalypse together with social action, you've got some fertile ground for introspection and service! How do we address our worst apocalyptic fears? More importantly, how do we address them with hope and promise so that all people reap the blessings?

This week, we'll look for the zombies in our lives, strive to live with the hope of the prophets, and see where we can bring a prophetic word to the little apocalypses of our time.

Day 1

Where are the zombies/locust in your life? What blessing will be waiting when they are gone?

The Study

Day 2

Who is your favorite prophet? If you see something today that reminds you of him/her, take a picture of it and journal here about what it means to you.

_____
_____
_____
_____
_____
_____
_____
_____
_____
_____
_____
_____

Day 3

Have you ever joined a prophetic activity–perhaps a religious or political march? What made the most impression on you?

The Study

Day 4

Joel is speaking to the community of Israel and Peter translates the words for the new community of Christians. How does your spiritual community live out these words of prophecy?

Day 5

What prophetic words of challenge and hope can you bring to the people around you?

The Study

Spiritual Action in Daily Life

Week Four

*Pilate asked him, 'So you are a king?'
Jesus answered, 'You say that I am a king. For this I was born,
and for this I came into the world, to testify to the truth.
Everyone who belongs to the truth listens to my voice.'
Pilate asked him, 'What is truth?'
After he had said this, he went out to the Jews again and told them,
'I find no case against him.' - John 18:37-38 (NRSV)*

Meditation

This week, our study focuses around truth – particularly the "truth within" scripture as opposed to the "truth of" scripture. Truth is a powerful topic in John's gospel; you might want to use a search engine like the one at bible.oremus.org and search for the many ways John uses the term.

There are even more verses using the word "truth" if you search all of scripture – 88, including the ones in the Apocrypha. And while that's nothing compared to the number of verses that include caring for the poor, the widow, the orphan, and the stranger– or the ones promoting justice – it is still a significant number!

John's approach to the truth is that it is contained in Jesus, not in any particular set of words or actions, but in the life, death, and resurrection of a man who was the Word, the Way, the incarnation of God.

That version of truth has some strong implications for the way Christians should live, according to John: in the image of Christ, who is the image of God.

So this week, we'll be looking at how truth affects us, what it requires of us, and how it empowers us to live a more truth-filled life.

The Study

Day 1

It's time for some truth-telling, truth-living, truth-processing: How often do you lie? Is it a rare event, an occasional occurrence, a way of life, an addiction?

Day 2

Look around you: what is the most "true" thing you see? Is it a fact – like gravity or oxygen – something that is absolute? Or is it a process, a way of living? Can you describe something here that depicts truth?

The Study

Day 3

The "truth within" reminds me of the prize at the bottom of a Cracker Jack box! Have you found truth anywhere unexpected lately?

Day 4

When you consider John's gospel in light of the idea of Jesus as "truth," does it change your ideas about discipleship? For example, if Jesus is truth and we are his body on earth, what are we to be?

The Study

Day 5

If you were going to live a new truth this weekend, what would it be?

Spiritual Action in Daily Life

Week Five

*I am a stranger and an alien residing among you;
give me property among you for a burying-place,
so that I may bury my dead out of my sight. - Genesis 23.4 (NRSV)*

The Study

Meditation

This week's study is about immigration - a story line that resonates throughout scripture!

Abraham left his homeland behind and traveled on to a land God promised him, losing much along the way but also gaining much!

Generations later, Joseph left that land and, years later, brought his family to him in Egypt. Generations after that, their descendants traveled back to the Promise Land.

A millennium later, Jesus echoed it when he called himself a stranger and the author of Hebrews wrote that all the faithful are strangers on earth.

And so the theme of being immigrants, being strangers in a strange land, is woven throughout the Bible. Odd how many religious people forget that, isn't it?

Because when we read these stories, we have to hear our own travelogue, too, don't we? The places in which we have been and the ways we've felt like, or been treated like, strangers in a strange land.

Whether we are immigrants or the descendants of immigrants, or those displaced by immigrants – literally or spiritually – we share in the story of strangeness. But we also share in the matching story of hospitality – of welcoming in people at all stages of their lives.

This week, we'll reflect on that a little as we consider how we might treat our fellow immigrants a little better, how we might be better strangers ourselves, and how we might take steps in the world on behalf of hospitality.

The Study

Day 1

Where are you "from"? How did you get to where you are now? How does your story resonate with the stories of other immigrants?

_____
_____
_____
_____
_____
_____
_____
_____
_____
_____
_____
_____
_____
_____
_____

Day 2

A friend told me how frightened he is during his monthly check-in at the Immigration & Customs Enforcement Center (ICE). Are there any places you go that make you afraid? What would it feel like if someone went there with you?

The Study

Day 3

In Matthew 25, Jesus told the "sheep" that when he was a stranger, they welcomed him while the "goats" did not. Do you see any strangers you can welcome? How does that feel?

_____
_____
_____
_____
_____
_____
_____
_____
_____
_____
_____
_____
_____
_____
_____

Day 4

Have you ever welcomed a stranger? Or fed someone who was hungry, visited someone in prison, gave someone thirsty a drink of water? Are there ways you can do that today?

_____

_____

_____

_____

_____

_____

_____

_____

_____

_____

_____

_____

_____

_____

_____

The Study

Day 5

How might you make hospitality a priority this weekend?

THE STUDY
Spiritual Action in Daily Life

Week Six

So I say to you, Ask, and it will be given to you;
search, and you will find;
knock, and the door will be opened for you. - Luke 11:9 (NRSV)

The Study

Meditation

A year or so ago, a friend told me about the scriptures he had memorized as a child – particularly Luke 11:10 and John 3:16 – scriptures about open doors and world-wide love.

Unfortunately, as a gay man, he quickly found out that the very people who taught him those verses, slammed the doors of the church in his face and denied he could experience the love of God.

And then, just when he thought no church would accept him, he met a pastor and some members of a spiritual community that invited him in, cared for him, and kept him connected.

They valued his life and his gifts and made him part of the community. They put their words into actions and became a significant part of his life.

Too often we forget that we have to say what we mean and mean what we say. We have to put life to our faith – to do what The Study is meant to help us do: take Spiritual Action in Daily Life!

This week, we are going to focus on what it means when the things we say match (or don't match) the things we do, on inclusion and exclusion, and on being pulled in and being sent away.

Day 1

What brought you to your spiritual community for the first time? Was a sense of authenticity part of it? What has/is/ might keep you there?

_____
_____
_____
_____
_____
_____
_____
_____
_____
_____
_____
_____
_____
_____
_____

The Study

Day 2

Did you ever memorize a Bible verse as a child (or adult)? What did people tell you it meant? Does it mean the same to you now? Why?

_____

_____

_____

_____

_____

_____

_____

_____

_____

_____

_____

_____

_____

Day 3

Are there places where you or those you love have been excluded for one reason or another? How do you cope with that? How does your faith help (or not) in coping or understanding?

The Study

Day 4

If you see a place where a door has been shut to others – or where one has been/could be opened, take a picture today and describe it here.

_____
_____
_____
_____
_____
_____
_____
_____
_____
_____
_____
_____
_____
_____
_____

Day 5

This weekend, look around you for places where what is said and done match or don't match. And list here any scriptures that could support or motivate you to make or encourage a change.

The Study

Spiritual Action in Daily Life

Week Seven

I am the good shepherd.
The good shepherd lays down his life for the sheep.
- John 10:11 (NRSV)

Meditation

There are so many scriptures related to shepherds! It's not just the verses about Jesus in the gospels but it's a thread that winds back throughout the Hebrew scriptures.

Think about how frequently they show up in Christian art! In stained glass windows, in paintings, in music, in stories – everything from bathrobe-encrusted children at Christmas to lamb-bearing storybook images of Jesus!

One of the important things we should remember about shepherds (but often forget) was that they were nomads, in conflict from the beginning with the more settled farmers.

They were less wealthy, less polished, less admirable – and more than a little anonymous! Yet God chose to use their love for the sheep in their care as an emblem for God's own love for the creation in God's care.

It reminds me of theologian Karl Rahner, who coined the phrase "Anonymous Christian." He wrote that:

> "Anonymous Christianity means that a person lives in the

The Study

> grace of God and attains salvation outside of explicitly constituted Christianity."

Someone who may never even have known Christianity, according to Rahner, could live within the grace of God... and equally, someone who does not know Christianity could show the face of Christ to someone else.

This week, we're going to think about those anonymous shepherds... and where we might find them in today's world... and how they might show us God's grace.

Day 1

In Jesus' day, a shepherd was someone who lived most of their life alone in the fields – rarely talking to anyone but their sheep. Who do you talk to when you're alone?

The Study

Day 2

Sheep like knowing their shepherd's presence and follow more closely when they can hear the shepherd's voice. Whose voices do you follow? Singers, politicians, artists, religious leaders, authors, pundits, comedians, etc.? How do they reflect God's voice to you?

_____

_____

_____

_____

_____

_____

_____

_____

_____

_____

_____

_____

_____

Day 3

Have you ever been to a secular art event and heard God's voice through an artist or their art?

The Study

Day 4

Sometimes we get a little nervous about hearing voices, etc. What is there that helps you be clear about what is God's voice, what is your own voice, and what might be a voice that could lead you astray?

Day 5

Do you live your faith anonymously? Why? What could make you less anonymous in the world this weekend?

The Study

Spiritual Action in Daily Life

Week Eight

*Taking the five loaves and the two fish, he looked up to heaven,
and blessed and broke the loaves,
and gave them to his disciples to set before the people;
and he divided the two fish among them all.
And all ate and were filled;
and they took up twelve baskets full
of broken pieces and of the fish.
Those who had eaten the loaves numbered five thousand men.
- Mark 6:41-44 (NRSV)*

Meditation

Recently a friend at church told me about her work for reproductive justice. It's a topic that is "hot" in so many ways and the longer we talked the more I understood how layered and complicated the feelings are around what it means to have justice in the area of reproductive rights.

What is reproductive justice to adults who could have been aborted as children because of mental or physical impairment?

To those of gender diversity whose parents might have chosen to abort them?

To a pregnant woman who's life is at risk – in any of a variety of ways?

To a supportive or non-supportive father-to-be?

To parents hearing that their unborn child will have horrific pain and suffering in a very short life?

My friend brought up this week's scripture to describe her social justice approach to reproductive justice: the story of the "loaves and fishes." It's a familiar story to many but applying it to social justice may be a fresh read for you! You can find the story told in all four of

The Study

the gospels, with some differences: Matthew 14:13-21, Mark 6:31-44, Luke 9:10-17 and John 6:5-15.

And this week, we'll think about ways we might be able to multiply our resources so that the many perspectives on this topic (and others) can each be treated with justice and grace, action and compassion.

Day 1

Have you ever had a conversation about reproductive justice that affected your thinking? How? What conversation today might bring you more new perspectives?

The Study

Day 2

Perspectives on this topic vary widely: as you meet people today, consider what reproductive justice might mean in their lives. How might that affect your view?

Day 3

Where do justice and grace, action and compassion intersect in your life? How might you need more resources to provide needed justice and action?

The Study

Day 4

If you find yourself in a place today where you could multiply resources to feed a hunger for justice, take a picture and describe it here as a way to remember to take that action in the future.

_____
_____
_____
_____
_____
_____
_____
_____
_____
_____
_____
_____
_____

Day 5

Sometimes we avoid discussing topics like this where there are so many perspectives and all of them may have some validity. Where could you venture into deeper dialogue on any of them?

The Study

Spiritual Action in Daily Life

Week Nine

*First of all, then,
I urge that supplications, prayers,
intercessions, and thanksgivings
should be made for everyone,
for kings and all who are in high positions,
so that we may lead a quiet and peaceable life
in all godliness and dignity. - 1 Timothy 2:1-2 (NRSV)*

Meditation

In a conversation with two women, both recently graduated seminary students, I listened to their thoughts about doing ministry in a local church.

In the process, they helped me to recover something of value in a scripture I had long ago given up on: 1Timothy, Chapter 2. The chapter's bold sexism, interpreted by so many men of prior generations to deny women a role among the clergy, just made me cringe!

But our conversation helped me remember that even losing a bit of scripture means losing a lot! They also reminded me that if I don't want to turn over responsibility for interpretation to others, then I have to do that work myself.

So after we talked, I reread J. Christiaan Beker's book, *Heirs of Paul*. Chris was one of my favorite professors in seminary - a complicated and difficult man who challenged and inspired me in every course!

Rereading that book reminded me that even in those early years after Paul, the church was already reinterpreting his writings for new times and new situations!

The Study

Reinterpreting is similar to what we've been doing for the past eight weeks in The Study: reinterpreting scriptures to find a way to live them out in your daily life.

Now, as this devotional book is coming to an end, let's turn our eyes forward. Let's see what you can reinterpret this week that can allow you to continue on in your study in the days and weeks, months and years, to come!

Day 1

The author of 1st Timothy was reinterpreting Paul for a new time. Is there a teacher from your past who you can reinterpret for your future?

The Study

Day 2

The author of 1st Timothy wrote about the need to keep silent. Can we reinterpret silence in a more positive way? Is there a way to build community through silence?

_____

_____

_____

_____

_____

_____

_____

_____

_____

_____

_____

_____

Day 3

What is/are your least favorite scripture/s? Is there a new way you can read in order to reclaim it/them? How could that help you to do your ministry?

The Study

Day 4

If you could reinterpret the traditions of your faith community, what could you do in ministry there? What new avenues of faith might open up for you, for them, for the world? Dream big!

_____
_____
_____
_____
_____
_____
_____
_____
_____
_____
_____
_____
_____
_____

Day 5

Follow up on this week's thoughts with a plan for rereading/reinterpreting in a way that will support your faith, build your ministries, and reach your dreams.

www.ingramcontent.com/pod-product-compliance
Lightning Source LLC
Chambersburg PA
CBHW021023090426
42738CB00007B/884